The Exceptional Leader
A Quick Guide to Personal Branding and
Leadership Development

Millette Granville

authorHOUSE®

AuthorHouse™
1663 Liberty Drive
Bloomington, IN 47403
www.authorhouse.com
Phone: 1-800-839-8640

First published by AuthorHouse 8/31/2010

ISBN: 978-1-4520-4122-3 (sc)
ISBN: 978-1-4520-4124-7 (e)

Library of Congress Control Number: 2010911880

Printed in the United States of America

This book is printed on acid-free paper.

Contents

Special Acknowledgment

I would like to acknowledge and thank Mr. Roderick Jackson for his patience and partnership in serving as the project editor for this book! Rod, it was a pleasure working with you on this project. You truly helped me to capture the essence of the message I want to deliver in this book. You have a wonderful gift and I am so glad we had an opportunity to collaborate on this project. Thank you!

Introduction

Though I have not always considered myself one, in retrospect, I now realize I have always embodied several key characteristics of an effective leader—a sense of responsibility, a proactive nature, the ability to listen and respect, and a healthy pursuit of personal excellence. My vocation of public speaking was a natural transition following my hard-earned successes as an entrepreneur, civic leader, and now my current role as a corporate executive.

From my public speaking appearances throughout the country to various professional conferences and business seminars on leadership and branding, there has been one constant request from those attending: "Where is your book?" Attendees requested a tangible reference guide on personal branding and leadership. Such humbling inquiries, my passion for personal development, coupled with the love and support from my parents made my decision to write this book an easy one. The numerous qualities that make for a dynamic leader are ones that my parents, Dr. George and Mattie Granville, instilled in me since birth. I cannot begin to measure the gratitude I feel towards them for their unwavering guidance, love, and support. My parents engrained in me the belief that a truly responsible person not only takes full accountability for one's actions but more, importantly, understands how these actions affect the lives of others.

With this premise in mind, I humbly submit to you this concise reference guide. It is not intended to serve as some magical branding and leadership elixir. However, this book will provide practical approaches to positively impact the brand that is you and to increase your ability to lead others.

Part 1: Personal Branding

At the risk of being cliché, "There is only one you." However, truly understanding and owning this fact is worth repeating the cliché. Knowing who you are, what you stand for, what motivates you, and what makes you special is the foundation of personal branding. We all have the power to be the next Oprah Winfrey if we choose to be.

Personal branding involves you taking the initiative to define yourself instead of allowing others to define you. Whether you are actively shaping your brand or not taking any steps whatsoever toward cultivating your personal or professional image, everyone has a brand that is either positive, negative, or somewhere in the middle. Currently, Oprah Winfrey and Tiger Woods are examples of personal brands on either end of the spectrum. From her talk show, which reaches millions, to her generous charity work to her financial supports of films with an uplifting message, Oprah has one of the strongest brands on our planet—a brand so strong that a single recommendation during her book club segment can turn an author into an instant best seller.

Golfer Tiger Woods had a brand just as powerful. However, unlike Oprah, Tiger failed to keep his brand consistent, which is essential for maintaining a strong brand. Overnight, Tiger's image went from that of a hard-working, driven, and highly respected family man who personified excellence to the butt of jokes due to numerous extra-marital affairs. As the dust continues to settle, Tiger has lost millions of dollars in endorsements from corporations who traded on his previous brand of goodness. Coupled with financial losses, he continues to suffer defeats in the court of public opinion. Again, the key to strong branding is consistency. If Tiger had had the womanizing "bad-boy" image of former professional basketball player Dennis Rodman or Gene Simmons of the rock group Kiss, there would have been little to no public uproar regarding Tiger's recent unsavory behavior. Granted, if this had been Tiger's original image, companies such as Gatorade, Accenture, and Tag Heuer would have never solicited his services as an endorser.

The key to a pronounced brand is self-awareness. Take a critical look at yourself and make an honest assessment of the image you project and its impact on others.

10 Ways to Build Your Personal Brand

1. Be authentic.
2. Have integrity.
3. Live and work in your passion.
4. Respect others and their time.
5. Always exceed expectations.
6. Keep your promises.
7. Build a diverse network.
8. Get involved, volunteer, and do special projects.
9. Take on a leadership role and be visible.

10. Know what you want to be famous for.

Be authentic

No one is as good at being you as you. Genuineness can be refreshing in the professional arena. Showcasing the "real" you allows you to exude calmness (as there is no extra effort required on your part) and in turn puts everyone around you more at ease. I have found that being authentic (while being respectful and tolerant) can be quite contagious. If you are not fond of the outdoors, it is not wise to volunteer to head a company whitewater rafting outing. Likewise, if you are in the midst of colleagues who tell demeaning jokes that you find offensive, laughing or continuing to remain in their presence will eat away at the core of who you proclaim to be. While compromise is essential to success, understand your areas of strength and weakness while standing firm on your basic values.

Have integrity

Integrity is fundamental to sustaining a strong personal brand. Once your integrity is breached, so is the trust and respect others had for you. The best opportunity one has to display integrity is often at a time when integrity can be easily compromised.

Live and work in your passion

Are you working for a purpose or a paycheck? You must discover your passion. Not society's passion, not a family member's passion, but your passion.

Once you truly discover it, you owe it to yourself to pursue this passion with extreme tenacity. Each day you work at a job that does not bring you joy, you not only cheat yourself out of true happiness and the pursuit of excellence, but you cheat your world out of your unique gifts. Granted, in these difficult economic times, mired with layoffs and cutbacks on educational funding, we often feel we are forced to work at jobs that do not bring any personal fulfillment but simply help make ends meet. This is a sad reality. However, even though you may find yourself in a situation that does not fit your passion, never lose sight of it. Allot some time each day to the pursuit of your desired goal—whether this entails researching your desired field or occupation online, taking preparatory classes, volunteering, applying for internships, or attending seminars. This consistent pursuit of your passion serves as a consistent internal reminder that your current position is a temporary one, and this continued effort and refusal to settle increases the chance that you will make a quicker transition into the position you desire.

Respect others and their time

Respect is a key component in creating and maintaining a reputable personal brand. The ability to show others they are valued is a trait every exceptional colleague and leader should possess. Never lose sight of the fact that in order to receive true respect, you must first show it. Once you have earned the respect of others, you will be privileged to enjoy their extreme effort and a much more positive environment.

One of the greatest displays of respect is punctuality. Not simple being on time but being early shows everyone involved that you hold your counterparts in high esteem and that you are serious and fully committed to the task at hand.

Always exceed expectations

I believe in this ideal so much that "Exceeding Your Expectations" was actually my company's slogan when I was president and CEO of Granville & Webb HR Connections, Inc., a human resources consulting firm. Because we now exist in such a highly competitive global marketplace, being average, or even good, just won't do. You must strive to be the best at all times. To do otherwise is to cheat the world of your intrinsic greatness, and more importantly, to cheat yourself. Author Marianne Williamson, in her book *Return to Love: Reflections on a Course in Miracles*, termed it best in her declaration that "our deepest fear is not that we are inadequate. Our deepest fear is that we are powerful beyond imagination. It is our light more than our darkness which scares us. We ask ourselves— who are we to be brilliant, beautiful, talented, and fabulous. But honestly, who are you to not be so?"

Keep your promises

Your word is one of the most crucial parts of your brand. Honoring your word engenders trust, respect, and confidence. It is critical, however, to infuse your lofty promises with a heavy dose of realism. In other words, never make promises you cannot keep.

Build a diverse network

Once you have accepted that you do not know it all—and neither do the people who look and think like you—you instantly become much smarter. As brilliant as we think we are, as humans we are limited. Even the most talented surgeon is usually limited in matters of law. Moreover, you may have the most innovative marketing plan to launch your product or service to the Chinese market. However, this effort will be increasingly difficult without a professional skilled in the Chinese language and culture. Building a diverse network is very important and surrounding yourself with people of a diverse background can help you appreciate and respect diversity.

Get involved and volunteer for special projects

Social and community volunteerism is a great way to demonstrate your passion for helping others and in turn adds credibility to your brand. It is beneficial to your brand to showcase that you believe in causes greater than yourself. From an altruistic standpoint, I have found that as you give, you actually *gain* more than you ever realize.

Volunteering for special projects on your job is an excellent way to demonstrate your unique talents and gifts. Also, this show of initiative gives others the opportunity to get to know you better and experience the value you add to the team.

Take on a leadership role and be visible

You can be the most talented, hardest working visionary in your organization, but if your abilities are not apparent to others, your skills will be wasted. As you build your brand at work and in your community, it is important to take on a leadership role and becoming increasingly visible. Many think that hard work is the only key to success; however, I now understand that visibility and exposure are just as important.

If your company or community is not soliciting for volunteers or leaders, it is incumbent upon you to take action and create visible opportunities to lead and volunteer. If people don't know your name and your abilities, they cannot call upon you or recommend you when that next great opportunity comes along. A person with a strong brand is not only well rounded but well known.

Know what you want to be famous for

Simply put, understand what you want to be remembered as and start working on it now! The sooner you know what you want to be famous for, the sharper your focus will become in terms of achieving those goals. This understanding will be a great aid in all phases of your life—from deciding what you want to do for a living to where you want to live to how you want to impact your community. You must take an honest assessment of yourself, identify your passion, work in your passion, and make every attempt to never compromise. This is the key to living your best life and building a strong and lasting personal brand.

Benefits of Creating a Strong Personal Brand

There are direct benefits that result from creating a strong personal brand.

- Position yourself clearly in the minds of others
- Project credibility
- Develop loyalty
- Make emotional connections

Position yourself clearly in the minds of others

With the increase of employment competition globally, the rise in the unemployment rate for corporate and academic America, along with technological advances that continually displace workers, it is critical to make yourself stand out in the thoughts and perceptions of others. If there was ever a time to ensure you do not appear mediocre or apathetic, it is now.

Project credibility

Credibility is a process, not an attribute achieved overnight. From the moment you enter an organization, you are being judged—even for something correctable, such as clothing or hairstyle. Therefore, as your time in the organization increases, it is solely up to you whether that judgment sways colleagues positively or negatively. When you look and act the part of a change agent, all while being professional, authentic, honest, and a problem-solver, your credibility will soar.

Develop loyalty

Leave no doubt that you are dedicated to the mission of your current project specifically and your organization as a whole. However, loyalty is a two-way street, in that it is essential for both the employee and the executive. From a management standpoint, James Allen, a nineteenth-century writer, phrased it best: "You do not attract what you wish. You attract what you are." Therefore it is incumbent upon entrepreneurs and corporate managers who want to attract the loyal and dedicated employees to display trustworthiness and loyalty themselves.

Make emotional connections

As we increasingly spend more time at the workplace than we do with our own families, we should make the work experience as pleasant as possible. Remember co-workers' names, and be curious about their hobbies and interests to foster a more tolerable work experience.

Creating Your Personal Brand Statement

Only you can develop, build, and sustain your brand. Your brand is as unique as your fingerprint. Building your brand is a lifetime commitment. A strong personal brand will last even after you are gone.

To determine exactly who you are, what you represent, and what unique talents gifts you bring to the world, it is extremely beneficial to begin this process of self-awareness by creating a personal brand statement. This exercise will prove to be quite self-revealing and therapeutic, as it affords you a unique opportunity to make an honest assessment of yourself. In preparing this statement, focus on who you are at your core, not what others may think of you (for the good or the bad), for others are often incorrect. We spend most of our lives allowing other people to define who we are, never taking the time to define (or redefine) ourselves. When thinking about my personal brand statement, I wanted it to stand as true today as it will be forty years from now. I believe that the legacy you leave should be the legacy you live. Therefore, it is my belief that you should live your personal brand statement each and every day.

Although there is power in the spoken word, the written word carries with it even more tangible credibility. This is because if you write something down you become accountable to it. In this section I will walk you through the process of creating your own personal brand statement.

My statement is simple and direct, yet it represents the true me:

> *Millette Granville is an energetic, giving, intelligent, spiritual, and passionate person. She has a spirit of excellence and believes anything worth doing is worth doing right. Millette believes that helping others is the greatest gift of all and one of her favorite quotes is from Gaudi: "We must be the change in the world we wish to see."*

The ability to connect inwardly with yourself is the initial step to creating your genuine personal brand statement. I found that an excellent path to inner enlightenment is through the practice of self-reflection, or meditation. I understand that many of those who consider themselves "movers and shakers" may be reluctant to participate in such a transcendental exercise. However, as a Type A personality myself, this practice was critical to understanding my true self and therefore being able to compose a pure, personal brand statement. The key step of this self-reflection process is finding a place of solitude where you can relax with no interruptions. I found that soothing music helped me clear my mind, relax, and focus deeply and inwardly.

For those not familiar with meditation techniques, the first thing you should do is sit up straight and roll your shoulders back to their natural and relaxed state. Next, close your eyes, take a deep breath, hold it for a few seconds, and then exhale slowly. Continue this breathing technique at least ten times and you will feel your body and mind starting to relax. During this exercise, purposefully remove all stressful and negative thoughts from your consciousness. If you feel your mind wondering (which is very likely to happen), refocus your concentration, again remove all interfering thoughts, focus on your breathing, and you will once again regain focus and return to a state of deep relaxation. You may find meditation difficult initially, and perhaps even fruitless, but I implore you to stick with it. I started meditating for merely two or three minutes at a time before I became comfortable with the process. I now find it an invaluable process to self-awareness.

Once you have obtained the feeling of relaxation, began to think about who you are, what you stand for, and what your true passions are. Likewise, think about what you want others to know about you, regardless of how unorthodox you may feel. Your meditation or self-reflection can last only three or four minutes. After the process is complete, open your eyes and begin to quietly write your personal brand statement.

Testing Your Brand Statement

Once you have completed scripting your personal brand statement, the real work begins. Now begins the rigorous tasks of living up to your words, and in the process the even more challenging charge of having others view you as such as well.

I have discovered two phenomenal ways to test your personal brand statements. First, identify a friend or family member that you spend a considerable amount of time with, a person who is objective, astute and completely honest, as you need to deal with someone who will be frank and direct. Next, find a casual place to engage them in conversation, over lunch or dinner. Casually mention that you read a recent article entitled "People Speak Louder than Words," where the "author" asserted that most people can be summarized in three words. Then ask the person to describe you in three words. If by chance the person asks you why you are asking that question, keep things light, plead curiosity, and refer back to the article. Do not share the real reason for your inquisition. Once the person has offered you the three words, refer back to your personal brand statement and see if any of the words the person stated are words you used in your brand statement. If some of the words are identical or synonymous, then there is a good chance that other people actually perceive you the way you perceive yourself. If you find that the words are not close to anything in your brand statement, go back to the person and kindly seek clarification. For example, if the person used a word you would not have used to describe yourself, you can lightly inquire, "I noticed you used that word to describe me. Can you tell me why?" You don't want to get defensive, because this will not get you what you need, which is clarity. Once you receive clarity you can then determine if that is something you want to change or improve upon.

The second way to test your brand statement is to find a person you respect, such as co-worker, a professor, or a mentor, and ask the question, "If you had to introduce me to someone, what would you say?" The same rules apply: you should not share the true reason for your line of questioning. Some people don't really listen when someone is introducing them, as they are usually waiting for their turn to speak. An introduction can be a great sneak peek into the mind of the person making the introduction. The person introducing you can really relay to the stranger how you have affected their lives by the way they choose to introduce you. For example, if you were introducing your mentor to a person, you would likely use glowing terms to describe the importance of your mentor to you and how your mentor has affected your life.

Therefore, pay deliberately attention the next time a colleague or superior is introducing you to a new person. What the introducer says or does not say can speak volumes. If you find that the majority of people introducing use only your name, you should really stop and think about why that is. For example, suppose I were to say, "Jane, meet Tim. I go to school with him." If that is all I have to say about Tim, that is a good indication that Tim has had little impact on my life. However, suppose I said, "Tim, meet Jane. She is dynamic, a great problem solver, and when I met her she introduced me to the right people and my career has been greatly impacted by my relationship with her." What is the difference between those two introductions? One is an introduction the other is an *endorsement*.

Once the person you are speaking with makes the mock introduction, pay close attention to the words they use and write them down. Later, take those words and compare them to your brand statement and see if any of those words are similar to the way you described yourself in your brand statement. The same rules apply here as they did when you were testing your statement. If you find the words are similar, you are in good shape. However, if you find that some of the words used in the introduction are dissimilar, ask the person why they chose those words. The best gift we can give ourselves is clarification. You can't change something if you don't know it needs changing.

Staying on Brand

After you have completed your brand statement, I recommend that you print it out and place it somewhere you can see it on a regular basis. In this hectic world, it is important to have motivating and consistent words to keep us on course. For example, suppose you are in school or at work and someone or some circumstance really upsets you. In a fit of anger, you are prepared to act in a retaliatory manner that is completely outside your character. Taking several deep breaths, understanding the potential repercussions of rash behavior, and revisiting your brand statement can save your reputation:

I was once personally involved in an unsettling situation, but after reviewing my personal brand statement, I came to terms that people who anger us take power over us, and if we choose to react in an unsavory manner, they maintain that power. Your brand statement can remind you of who you are and prevent you from acting out of your true character. I firmly believe that just as I can create my own personal brand statement, I too can create my own destiny.

Notes.

Notes.

_____
_____
_____
_____
_____
_____
_____
_____
_____
_____
_____
_____
_____
_____
_____
_____
_____
_____
_____
_____
_____
_____
_____
_____
_____
_____
_____

Part 2: What Is the True Meaning of Leadership?

The true leader serves. Serves people. Serves their best interests, and in doing so will not always be popular, may not always impress. But because true leaders are motivated by loving concern than a desire for personal glory, they are willing to pay the price.
—Eugene B. Habecker

For me, the favorite definition of true leadership simple and straightforward—leadership is the art of motivating a group of people to strive toward a common goal. The leader is the inspiration and director of the action. He or she is the person in the group who possesses the combination of personality and skills that makes others want to follow his or her direction.

The 5 Core Principles of Leadership

The journey to exceptional leadership begins with five core principles.

1. Service
2. Trustworthiness
3. Engagement
4. Vision
5. Innovation

Service

One of the most admirable traits of an effective and respected leader is service. It is vital that these motivators of men and women believe in and dedicate their efforts to causes greater than themselves and their egos. This sense of service is also an excellent motivating tool, as it becomes contagious to others who work for the leader. There is no greater motivating force than being an active example of what you ask from others.

This spirit of service embodies a willingness to do everything required to foster the proper environment for growth, development, engagement, and profitability. A dynamic leader must possess an inner drive to help subunits and colleagues alike become the most productive yet fulfilled workers imaginable.

Great leaders make service a common practice in their daily lives. An exceptional leader makes it his or her duty to get to know the team members and clients. Leaders also make it a point to interact with the people in the community and industry, and they create an open-door policy so consistent communication is always there. If you are a new leader in your organization and you don't have direct reports, you can demonstrate your leadership by opening doors for others and by creating learning and development opportunities for your team members and community. It is your responsibility to find out what the needs of the people are and to create solutions that will meet them. To serve is to be selfless and to commit to enhancing the situation of those around you.

If you desire to be an exceptional leader, here are a few things you can do to be of service.

Understand your environment.

Communication styles, corporate structures, and overall business cultures vary from industry to industry, company to company, and city to city. Gain a clear understanding of the environment in which you work and adjust your approach accordingly.

Identify the needs of your company/community.

By identifying the needs of your company/community, you accomplish two things: (a) you place yourself in a much better position to eventually satisfy those needs, and (b) you set yourself apart as acute and efficient problem solver—abilities every organization admires and desires.

Develop a plan of action

Overall, it is not beneficial to point out the needs or problems at hand without the wisdom necessary to solve these issues. You must develop a plan, get buy-in from your team, and work the plan.

Articulate the plan and discuss the desired outcome.

A standout leader is able to tie in their vision with expected results. Concisely articulating the link between the plan and the outcome provides workers with not only a distinct roadmap but a stronger sense of purpose.

Provide necessary resources.

Two-time Super Bowl winning Coach Bill Parcells lamented that he was not involved enough in the New England Patriots' football personnel decisions. "If they want you to cook the dinner, at least they ought to let you shop for some of the groceries," he said. As a leader who expects excellence from your group, you must provide all the tools necessary for them to achieve that excellence.

Hold yourself and others accountable for their commitments.

One of the strongest ways for you as a leader to command loyalty and supreme effort from others is to avoid placing expectations on others that you would not place on yourself. Leading by example never gets old.

Stay connected.

A leader must understand what motivates and, conversely, deflates others. The more in tune you are with the thoughts and desires of others, the quicker you can adjust your leadership style to adjust to varying situations and individuals.

Trustworthiness

Depend upon yourself. Make your judgment trustworthy by trusting it. You can develop good judgment as you do the muscles of your body—by judicious, daily exercise. To be known as a man of sound judgment will be much in your favor.

—Grantland Rice

Before you can you can gain the trust of others, you must first trust yourself. And to trust yourself, you need to understand yourself. This means you must know who you are, show who you are, and be unwavering in keeping your word. This does not happen overnight, as trust is only achieved through time and consistency. However, through your life experiences and continued decision-making opportunities, you will eventually come to become confident in your own judgment and wisdom.

To become a great leader you must be committed to building teams and relationships through trust and authentic concern for those you impact. There are several essential factors you must adhere to in establishing trust with others.

- Develop your character, for it will determine your credibility.
- Be great at your job and exceed expectations.
- Be a leader of great influence.
- Don't make promises you can't keep.
- Foster honest and direct communication.
- Speak your mind respectfully.
- Always respect the opinions and thoughts of others.
- Have your team's (or community's) best interest at heart in all that you do.

- Demonstrate your concern often.
- Be action oriented and results focused.
- Don't be self-serving.

When others trust you they will believe in you and thus follow you, making your goals much more achievable.

Engagement

To be an engaging leader you must demonstrate, through your attitude and actions that you genuinely care about the people you work with and serve. The people you are leading must believe that you have their best interests at heart. Here are some ways you can become more engaging with your team.

- Get to know your team.
- Show that you are committed to and invested in your team's success.
- Be thoughtful and take time to ask how they are doing.
- Demonstrate concern for what is happening in their personal lives.
- Engage in small talk before you get down to business.
- Let your team see who you really are.
- Share your excitement and concerns with your team.
- When possible, incorporate team outings and off-sites to engage the team.
- Identify a mentor for yourself

It pays to be emotionally invested in your team/ community. When people see that you care, they will return the favor by caring for you and your vision. Being an engaging leader allows you to build strong solid relationships and make a difference. A team that believes their leader cares about them is a team that performs at the highest level.

Vision

Good business leaders create a vision, articulate the vision, passionately own the vision, and relentlessly drive it to completion.

—Jack Welch

I believe in the adage, "Without vision, the people will perish." In your quest to become an exceptional leader, you must see the vision, own the vision, articulate the vision, and make the vision a reality.

The following are essential components in facilitating your vision as a leader:

Take a moment of silence.

As previously discussed, do not be afraid of silence. In our current environment, where we are constantly inundated with smartphones, laptops, and a 24-hour news cycle, quiet reflection is an excellent way to hone in on your vision. As the leader, you have to be committed and convinced that your vision is valid and achievable, and there is nothing like honest and peaceful reflection to confirm this is true.

Be transformational, not transactional.

Today's ever-changing work environment calls for a leader who is able to transform the current environment by envisioning new possibilities that are increasingly less defined. The leader needs to be able to discuss possibilities and acknowledge the challenges, viewing them as opportunities and not barriers. Transformational leaders must understand what needs to be changed and be able to put a plan together to make the transition a reality.

Don't let your circumstances define your outcome.

Great leaders must see beyond the current state and into the future. A true leader must be able to get others to buy into their shared vision, so that positive change can occur. When adversity arises in your organization, you must have the temperament to assess the situation from a dispassionate standpoint, and then begin making sound, rational decisions that will lead your group out of this negative situation.

Celebrate the small victories.

Although many managers show recognition only upon completion of the project or goal, a responsive leader acknowledges and rewards their staff for positive achievements along various steps of the journey. This consistent acknowledgement fosters a more engaged and appreciative workforce throughout the process. There is a direct correlation between showing those you are proud of their superior work and the likelihood such superior work will continue.

Innovation

Without change there is no innovation, creativity, or incentive for improvement. Those who initiate change will have a better opportunity to manage the change that is inevitable.

—William Pollard

Change is the one constant in our lives, and it therefore is up to us to embrace change and forge ahead, lest we resist change and be left behind. Therefore, to be an effective leader one must be an innovator. As our world becomes increasingly smaller due to technology and communication, innovative methods to reach business goals (or solve societal problems) are vital. As leader, you must constantly discover creative methods for improving your business, the community, and the lives of others.

To be an innovator is to be daring, to be bold and to be without the fear to fail. Failure is the best way for us to perfect our craft. Sometimes innovation requires someone who is not only willing to think outside the box but willing to take the entire box apart if necessary. An innovator understands that the seemingly impossible is possible, with imagination, knowledge, and good old-fashion hard work. True innovators do not carry the burden of change and advancement alone. They encourage all involved to become creative thinkers and problem solvers. They inspire all to think the unthinkable, to believe the unbelievable, and to achieve the unachievable.

Regardless of how often your employees' ideas succeed, as a leader you must continue to encourage workers to provide suggestions on subjects such as improving efficiency, production, service, and employee quality of life. Encouraging and rewarding employees for presenting innovative ideas will foster an environment where the employees feel more valued and will therefore continue to offer plans that will benefit your organization.

Notes.

_____
_____
_____
_____
_____
_____
_____
_____
_____
_____
_____
_____
_____
_____
_____
_____
_____
_____
_____
_____
_____
_____
_____
_____
_____
_____
_____

Notes.

Part 3: Becoming an Exceptional Leader

The 6 Characteristics of an Exceptional Leader

Once the core principles of leadership are achieved, one should look to move to the next level by embracing six characteristics that are necessary for exceptional leadership.

Integrity

With corporate and political entities mired in and often destroyed by corrupt leadership, being leader with integrity is now more important than ever. If your people do not believe you and if your actions are illegal and immoral, it is impossible to command the respect needed to be a prominent leader. Having integrity means being always truthful, supportive, and determined to do what is right. It means that if you say you will do something, you will go to great lengths to get it done. Integrity truly means that people can always count on you to deliver on what you promised. You cannot lead effectively in the workplace, at home, or in your community if you are unable to exemplify honor and integrity.

To demonstrate integrity, you must do the following:

- Be honest.
- Be transparent.
- Be consistent.
- Be dependable.
- Be open and flexible.

Optimism

A pessimist sees the difficulty in every opportunity; an optimist sees the opportunity in every difficulty.
—Winston Churchill

Great leaders not only see and take advantage of opportunities but have the fortitude to create an opportunity if one does not appear. People will not wholeheartedly follow someone who is shortsighted, complaining about his current situation. A strong leader will let people vent for a few minutes but then move right into action mode to change the situation at hand. As a leader, it is not just your job but your obligation to effect change through a positive attitude and an open mind. As you lead your team/community, it is your job to make sure the team does not embrace or encourage those who refuse to see the possibility and only want to focus on the negative. To do this you must provide options and an environment that promotes creativity. With the willingness to change and the tools to change, anything is possible.

Risk taker

During these volatile economic times, marked by corporate downsizing, teacher layoffs, and governmental budget cuts, taking measured risks has become increasingly essential for the survival of an organization. However, before a risk is assumed, a leader should always fully evaluate the potential outcome from both a positive and negative standpoint. The leader must also determine the repercussions if the outcome is negative. It is only through true risks that rewards are achieved; therefore, trial and error are the fundamentals of growth and success. The key is learning and building upon mistakes. As the leader you have to be able to foster this same attitude in the people you support. To be a calculated risk taker, you must be good at conducting research, finding creative ways to solve problems, and be able to implement a good plan to achieve your desired results.

Change agent

Leaders have to be committed to updating and improving their environments at all times. To achieve this, a leader must be comfortable with the change and be able to embrace and communicate its benefits to others. In order to be a great agent of change and an impactful leader, you must be completely committed to understanding the ever-changing business world/ community in which you live and work. You must accept that nothing stays the same and know that in order to grow and be more productive, you must always seek out new and innovative ways to effect change. Being a change agent is not always easy, because most people are naturally resistant to change. We are creatures of habit, and habits are usually hard to break. Articulating the vision and the value of the change is the most effective way to get the results you seek. If your team/community can buy into why the change is needed and how it will benefit them, they will help you execute your plan.

Motivator

The greater the loyalty of a group toward the group, the greater is the motivation among the members to achieve the goals of the group, and the greater the probability that the group will achieve its goals.
—Rensis Likert

Exceptional leaders are able to tap into others inward drive. It is therefore your task to comprehend what actually motivates each individual in your team and employ the proper tactics to bring out the best in them. Once a leader understands what motivates each team member, it is then the leader's responsibility to create proper rewards for those who achieve and exceed their respective goals. For those yet to achieve the desired goal, motivation can still play an integral part in urging a person to keep aiming higher.

People are motivated by a variety of factors, ranging from money and job flexibility to peer recognition. As a leader, although you can encourage, teach, and support, it is impossible to dictate how a person will respond to your efforts. Some leaders may mistakenly feel that having an energetic personality will translate to having an energetic staff. Energy is an excellent quality in a leader; however, although you may possess that quality, your team members may not. For example, you may be leading a group of highly skilled and productive accountants who, as a whole, lack outward energy and exuberance. However, these same accountants might maintain a high level of motivation to excel based on consistent recognition, flexible work hours, and performance bonuses. The leader should be astute enough to provide the necessary motivating resources to maintain excellence.

The motivation is only as good as the provisions made to meet the objectives at hand. A highly motivated team will always strive to exceed expectations because; meeting them will not be enough. The best way to motivate a team or people in your community is to first understand their needs, evaluate the project at hand, be able to clearly state the goals and objectives, supply the tools that are needed to get the job done, and lead by example.

Dedication

Exceptional leaders are dedicated to their teams, their community, and themselves. You cannot lead a team of people if you can't demonstrate to them that you too are invested in the cause you are promoting. Others have to see that no matter what happens, you are going to support them and make the decisions that will positively affect their lives. You must demonstrate true dedication in all your daily actions. You have to be dedicated to the cause constantly—through good times and bad. Consistency is the true key to demonstrating your dedication to the team and the work you have to do. Some of the ways to demonstrate your commitment include the following:

- Listen first.

- Understand second.
- Provide feedback.
- Be committed to providing resources to get the job done.
- Articulate the vision and the benefits.
- Follow up and follow through on the promises you make.
- Reward hard work and creativity.

Notes.

_____

_____

_____

_____

_____

_____

_____

_____

_____

_____

_____

_____

_____

_____

_____

_____

_____

_____

_____

_____

_____

_____

_____

_____

_____

_____

Notes.

Part 4: Pay It Forward

The true testament of exceptional leadership is the review after the leader is no longer present. The works and legacy of leaders such as King, Kennedy, Roosevelt, Carnegie, and Ghandi have far outlasted their natural lives. The best way to tell if a leader has truly made an impact on an organization or community is to look at what happens to their cause after that leader has moved on. It is our duty and our obligation to reach back and make sure we are training and developing future leaders. Some of us are great at leading and inspiring others to do the same, whereas others, sadly, are satisfied with being the only ones who receive the praise and credit.

Exceptional leaders are consumed with giving back and committed to finding the best ways to train, mentor, teach, reach, and develop future leaders on the job and in their community. Succession planning is the most effective way to pay it forward. You must identity people in your group or community who you think have what it takes to lead. Then you have to be committed to investing time, knowledge, and advice to make sure they are able to lead now and learn from their mistakes. There are five steps to helping others become great leaders.

The Five Ways to Help Others Become Great Leaders

1. Understand the people around you.
2. Recognize and embrace generational differences.
3. Create the right environment for learning and doing the work.
4. Promote continuous learning.
5. Serve as a mentor and a sponsor.

Understand the people around you

A prolific leader needs clear knowledge of those with whom they work. A leader must have a solid grasp of their team's strengths and weaknesses, as well as an understanding of what motivates and distracts.

Recognize and embrace generational differences

Regardless of age, each talented member of an organization brings value. Whether it is the energy and technological savvy of a newcomer or the wisdom and loyalty of a thirty-year employee, everyone's talents and contributions should be acknowledged and encouraged.

Create the right environment for learning and doing the work

An effective leader establishes a setting in which everyone can excel. This entails listening actively and thinking forwardly. Understanding the trends and changes in your particular industry is vital to long-term success.

Promote continuous learning

As the economy, technology, and laws change, so does your industry. It is therefore incumbent upon a leader to stay abreast of all industry-wide modifications, keeping their workforce educated, certified, and far beyond the curve.

Serve as a mentor and a sponsor

There is no better way to further the cause than by becoming a sponsor and a mentor to those eager to learn. It is important to understand the difference between a mentor and a sponsor. A mentor is someone you can go to on a casual basis to talk about your issues, ask for advice, and run ideas by. Your mentor can be a friend, coworker, or community member. A sponsor plays a different role in the development of others. You can usually identify a sponsor in the work environment. This is someone who stands in your corner and supports you when you are not in the room. Both mentors and sponsors are usually people with great influence and character, and therefore worth emulating. A close personal relationship with a sponsor is not required, but the relationship does have to be a respectful one.

A true leader will seek out opportunities to serve as a mentor and a sponsor to those they feel can and will become great leaders. The ability to affect the lives of others is truly a gift, and the more you put others first, the more satisfaction you as a leader will obtain.

Leadership and service is not a right but a privilege. Good leadership is about putting others first and performing all duties to the very best of your ability. Great leadership is leading by example. Exceptional leadership is about service, putting the needs of others before your own. Leadership involves being a visionary, investing in others, teaching, and reaching back to give back. There are many in power in our society, but there are few leaders. The powerful may have influence, but a leader has impact. The powerful can make changes, but a leader can change lives.

Notes.

Notes.

About the Author

Noted public speaker Millette Granville, vice president and diversity and college recruiting manager for a major financial services company, is a career expert and founder of S.P.E.A.K. (Speaking Professionally and Enthusiastically to Awaken Knowledge). Millette has conducted workshops and seminars on leadership and professional development, diversity, and personal branding. She has been a featured speaker for the following organizations: Wachovia Bank, a Wells Fargo Company, the National Black MBA Association, the National Urban League of Central Carolinas, the National Association of African Americans in Human Resources, NAACP Leadership Summit, Winston Salem State University, Winthrop University, Hampton University, MEAC Women's Athletic Leadership Conference, Central Intercollegiate Athletic Association (CIAA) Student Athletes, Employment Management Association of SHRM, and the Charlotte Chapter of Black Journalists. She has over twenty years of experience in corporate diversity and recruiting. For five years she was president/CEO of Granville & Webb HR Connections Inc., a human resources consulting and executive search firm. Millette has been featured in the following magazines: *The National Black MBA Magazine*, *Diversity Woman Magazine*, *Diversity Edge Magazine*, *Working Charlotte Magazine*, and the *Careers & disABLED Magazine*. Millette is passionate about using her knowledge and skills to help others become more effective leaders.

millette.granville@speakmg.com

LaVergne, TN USA
16 September 2010
197187LV00006B/5/P